Beyond Belief

Discovering Sacred Moments in Everyday Life

Dan Desmarques

22 Lions

Beyond Belief: Discovering Sacred Moments in Everyday Life

Written by Dan Desmarques

Copyright © 2024 by Dan Desmarques. All Rights Reserved.

No part of this publication may be reproduced or transmitted in any form or by any means, electronic or mechanical, including photocopy, recording, or any information storage and retrieval system now known or to be invented, without permission in writing from the publisher, except by a reviewer who wishes to quote brief passages in connection with a review written for inclusion in a magazine, newspaper, or broadcast.

Contents

Introduction	VII
1. Chapter 1: The Nature of God	1
2. Chapter 2: God and Spirituality	5
3. Chapter 3: The Role of Faith	9
4. Chapter 4: God and Human Emotions	13
5. Chapter 5: The Divine Within	17
6. Chapter 6: God and the Universe	21
7. Chapter 7: The Illusion of Separation	25
8. Chapter 8: God and Suffering	29
9. Chapter 9: The Power of Prayer	33
10. Chapter 10: God and Morality	37
11. Chapter 11: The Pursuit of Truth	41
12. Chapter 12: God and Human Potential	45
13. Chapter 13: The Nature of Evil	49
14. Chapter 14: God and Community	53
15. Chapter 15: The Transformative Power of Love	57

16.	Chapter 16: Life After Death	61
17.	Chapter 17: The Language of God	65
18.	Chapter 18: God and Personal Responsibility	69
19.	Chapter 19: The Future of Spirituality	73
20.	Chapter 20: Embracing the Divine	77
21.	Glossary of Terms	81
22.	Book Review Request	87
23.	About the Author	89
24.	Also Written by the Author	91
25.	About the Publisher	101

Introduction

"Beyond Belief: Discovering Sacred Moments in Everyday Life" invites you on a transformative journey into the heart of spirituality, transcending religious boundaries and illuminating the universal essence of the divine. This engaging and insightful guide is a beacon for seekers who want to deepen their understanding of the sacred and cultivate a more meaningful spiritual life.

Why this book will resonate with you

- Drawing on timeless wisdom from diverse cultures and faiths, Divine Explorations reveals the divine as a unifying force that connects us all, making it accessible and relevant to readers of all backgrounds.

- Personal Growth: By encouraging introspection and self-awareness, this book empowers you to forge a personal relationship with the divine, fostering spiritual growth and a profound sense of purpose.

- Emotional Depth: Delve into the intricate connection between human emotions and spiritual experience, uncovering the love and compassion that lie at the heart of the Divine.

- Practical Application: The book offers actionable insights and practices-from mindfulness and gratitude to connecting with nature and community-that enable you to integrate spirituality into your daily life.

- Celebrating the diversity of spiritual paths, this book promotes an inclusive perspective that emphasizes the common human search for meaning and connection.

What makes this book different?

- Holistic vision: Blending philosophical inquiry, spiritual teachings, and personal exploration, this book presents a comprehensive and engaging examination of the divine.

- Challenging and Inspiring: The book challenges conventional notions of God, inviting you to question, reflect, and ultimately grow in your spiritual understanding.

- Transformative: By emphasizing the interconnectedness of all things and the divine spark within each of us, this book has the power to transform your perception of yourself and the world around you.

"Beyond Belief: Discovering Sacred Moments in Everyday Life" is not just a book; it is an invitation to a richer, more fulfilling spiritual life. Prepare to be inspired, challenged, and transformed as you delve into the mysteries of the divine and embrace a deeper connection to the universal essence that connects us all.

Chapter 1: The Nature of God

The concept of God has been a central theme in human thought, transcending cultures, eras, and belief systems. At its core, the understanding of God is not limited to the teachings of organized religions, but extends to universal truths that resonate with the essence of existence. The divine is not limited by religious boundaries, but is a universal principle that governs the cosmos. As a universal truth, God embodies principles of love, compassion, and interconnectedness. This understanding is consistent with the notion that all beings are manifestations of a single divine essence. Various spiritual traditions converge on the idea that God is not an external entity to be worshipped from afar, but an intrinsic part of our being. This perspective invites individuals to recognize the divine in themselves and in others, fostering a sense of unity and common purpose.

Many religious texts describe God as a creator, a source of life, and a guiding force. However, interpretations of God vary widely from culture to culture. For example, monotheistic traditions often view God as a single, omnipotent being, while polytheistic beliefs represent the divine through multiple deities, each embodying different aspects of existence. Despite these differences, the underlying message remains consistent: God is a force that inspires, nourishes, and guides humanity toward higher consciousness.

The transcendence of God beyond religious boundaries is crucial to understanding the role of the divine in human life. Many people become disillusioned with organized religion, often because of rigid structures and dogmas that can hinder personal spiritual growth. This disillusionment can lead to a search for a more personal and direct relationship with the divine that is not mediated by religious institutions. In this context, spirituality becomes a journey of self-discovery in which individuals seek to connect with the divine through personal experience, meditation, and introspection.

In addition, the teachings of various spiritual leaders emphasize that the essence of God is love. This love is not conditional or transactional; it is an unconditional force that permeates all aspects of life. It is through love that individuals can transcend their limitations, heal emotional wounds, and foster deeper connections with others. Recognizing this divine love can lead to profound transformations, allowing individuals to break free from fear, resentment, and anger.

Exploring the nature of God also deepens our understanding of existence itself. Many philosophical and spiritual traditions propose that life is a manifestation of divine energy and that each experience serves a purpose in the grand tapestry of creation. This perspective encourages individuals to view challenges and adversity as opportunities for growth and learning. By embracing this mindset, one can cultivate a sense of purpose, recognizing that every moment is a chance to align with the divine will.

In addition, the interconnectedness of all beings is a fundamental aspect of understanding God. The idea that we are all part of a greater whole fosters a sense of responsibility to one another and to the planet. This interconnectedness is reflected in the teachings of various spiritual traditions, which emphasize the importance of compassion, empathy, and altruism. By recognizing the divine spark in others, individuals are inspired to act with kindness and understanding, contributing to a more harmonious world.

Chapter 2: God and Spirituality

While religion is often characterized by structured systems of belief, ritual, and doctrine, spirituality is more personal and subjective, embodying an individual's unique experience of the divine. This distinction is crucial to understanding how people relate to God and the universe, as it underscores the multifaceted nature of faith and existence.

Religion in its traditional form serves as a framework that provides guidelines for moral behavior, community belonging, and a sense of purpose. However, it can also become rigid, with dogma overshadowing personal experience. Many people feel constrained by religious expectations, resulting in a disconnect between their inner spiritual journey and the outer practices dictated by their faith. Here, spirituality offers a more fluid and dynamic approach to understanding God.

Spirituality invites individuals on a personal journey of discovery where the divine is not just an abstract concept, but a living reality experienced in daily life. It emphasizes the importance of personal spiritual experiences, which can take many forms-meditation, nature, art, or moments of profound insight. These experiences serve as gateways to a deeper understanding of self and the universe, allowing individuals to connect with the divine in ways that transcend traditional religious practices.

True spirituality is rooted in self-awareness and the recognition of one's inner desires and fears. A mind preoccupied with the constructs of the ego can overlook the profound possibilities of the soul's deepest longings. This disconnect can lead to a life of disappointment and missed opportunities, as the individual fails to acknowledge the success that is already present in his or her life, albeit in forms different from societal norms.

In addition, the dynamic nature of the personality significantly influences one's spiritual journey. Each individual experiences various pulls and pushes throughout life, driven by impulses related to belonging, security, and personal desires. However, it is the spiritual impulse-the innate drive to make lasting connections and recognize love-that ultimately leads to true happiness and fulfillment. This recognition is essential because it allows individuals to navigate life's complexities with a sense of purpose and direction.

The concept of sacrifice also emerges as a critical element in the spiritual journey. True sacrifice is not just about physical offerings or rituals; it involves a willingness to invest everything one has in the pursuit of a higher purpose, even at the cost of personal comfort. This level of commitment requires faith in the outcome and a willingness to embrace the unknown, which can be both daunting and liberating.

As individuals delve deeper into their spiritual paths, they often encounter existential dilemmas that challenge their values and beliefs. These moments serve as tests of faith, revealing hidden desires and fears. It is through confronting these inner struggles that one can experience profound transformation, leading either to a rebirth of spirit or a slow decline into despair.

Knowledge and wisdom are not simply acquired from external sources, but come from personal observation and recognition. Each unexpected encounter can serve as a lesson, leading individuals to a greater understanding of themselves and their place in the universe. This process of self-discovery is essential to spiritual growth and fosters resilience and adaptability in the face of life's challenges.

Ultimately, one's relationship with God is deeply personal and subjective, shaped by individual experiences and emotions. As one cultivates awareness and mindfulness, the divine presence becomes evident in the mundane aspects of life, transforming one's understanding of God from an abstract concept to a tangible reality. This shift in perception allows the individual to find God not only in sacred spaces, but also in the beauty of nature, the kindness of others, and the quiet moments of reflection.

Chapter 3: The Role of Faith

Faith serves as a profound guiding force in the lives of individuals, shaping not only their perception of the divine, but also their understanding of existence itself. It transcends mere belief and embodies trust, hope, and a deep-seated conviction of a greater purpose. This exploration of faith reveals its transformative power and illustrates how it can light the way through life's uncertainties and challenges.

At its core, faith acts as an inner compass, guiding individuals toward their aspirations and desires. It is a belief in something greater than oneself that provides strength in times of adversity. This guiding principle allows individuals to navigate the complexities of life with a sense of purpose and direction. When faced with existential dilemmas, faith acts as a stabilizing force, enabling individuals to face their fears and uncertainties with courage. Faith is not merely passive acceptance; it is an active engagement with the world, a commitment to pursue one's dreams despite obstacles.

The relationship between faith and perception is particularly important. Faith shapes how individuals view God and the universe, influencing their understanding of existence and their place within it. For many, God is not just a distant entity, but a personal presence that guides and supports them. This perception fosters a sense of connection and belonging, allowing individuals to feel part of a larger tapestry of life. When one approaches life with faith, one is more likely to perceive the divine in everyday experiences and to recognize the sacred in the mundane.

In addition, faith encourages individuals to embrace the unknown. It invites them to step outside their comfort zone and explore new possibilities. This willingness to venture into the unknown is essential to personal growth and spiritual development. True faith is not blind; rather, it is rooted in a deep understanding of oneself and the universe. It recognizes that life is a journey filled with lessons and that each experience, whether positive or negative, contributes to one's spiritual development.

In this context, faith also plays a critical role in shaping one's values and moral compass. It influences how individuals interact with others and the world around them. A strong foundation of faith often leads to a greater sense of compassion, empathy, and altruism. When individuals perceive the divine in others, they are more likely to act with kindness and understanding. This interconnectedness fosters a sense of community and belonging, reinforcing the idea that we are all part of a greater whole.

However, when faith is rooted in dogma or rigid belief systems, it can lead to division and conflict. True faith should be flexible and open to evolution. It should encourage individuals to question, explore, and seek deeper understanding, rather than cling to fixed beliefs that may no longer serve them. This adaptability is essential for spiritual growth, as it allows individuals to evolve in their understanding of and relationship with the divine.

Moreover, the transformative power of faith is often revealed in moments of crisis. In difficult times, individuals may struggle with doubt and uncertainty. It is in these moments that faith can either falter or flourish. When individuals face their fears and embrace their vulnerabilities, they often emerge stronger and more resilient. This process of facing adversity with faith can lead to profound personal transformation, allowing individuals to discover their inner strength and potential.

Chapter 4: God and Human Emotions

The complex relationship between human emotions and spiritual experience is a profound aspect of our existence. Emotions are not just fleeting feelings; they are the essence of our connection to the Divine. As we explore the nature of God, we find that love and compassion are not just attributes, but fundamental characteristics that reflect the divine essence itself.

At the heart of the human experience is the emotion of love. Love transcends mere affection; it is a powerful force that binds us to one another and to the universe. It is through love that we experience the divine presence in our lives. When we love, we tap into a higher frequency of existence, one that resonates with the very fabric of creation. This connection is not limited to romantic love, but extends to family bonds, friendships, and even the love we feel for strangers. Each act of love is a reflection of the divine, a glimpse into the heart of God, who embodies unconditional love.

Compassion, which is closely related to love, serves as a bridge between our human experiences and the Divine. It is the ability to empathize with others, to feel their pain and joy, and to respond with kindness. Compassion is a divine quality that calls us to action to alleviate suffering and uplift those around us. In moments of compassion, we become vessels of God's grace, channeling divine energy into the world. This act of selflessness not only transforms the lives of others, but also enriches our own spiritual journey, allowing us to grow closer to the Divine.

The teachings of various spiritual traditions emphasize the importance of love and compassion as pathways to understanding God. For example, many religious texts emphasize that to know God is to love, and to love is to serve. This service often manifests itself in acts of kindness, charity, and understanding toward others. When we engage in these acts, we align ourselves with the divine will, creating a ripple effect that can transform communities and societies.

In addition, the emotional landscape of humanity is often characterized by fear, anger, and resentment. These emotions can cloud our perception of the divine and lead us to believe in a punishing rather than a loving God. It is important to recognize that these negative emotions are not inherent in our nature, but are often products of our environment and experiences. By cultivating love and compassion, we can transcend these limitations and reconnect with the divine essence that resides within us.

The journey to spiritual enlightenment requires that we face our fears and insecurities, embrace vulnerability, and allow ourselves to be transformed by love. This transformation is akin to a rebirth in which we shed the layers of ego and self-doubt that hinder our connection to God. In the process, we learn that our worth is not determined by external validation, but by our ability to love and be loved.

As we navigate through life, it is important to remember that every emotion we experience serves a purpose. Joy, sorrow, anger, and love are all integral to our spiritual growth. They give us insight into our inner self and lead us to a deeper understanding of our relationship with the Divine. By embracing our emotions, we can cultivate a deeper connection with God and experience the fullness of life.

Our emotions are not mere reactions to external stimuli; they are sacred pathways that lead us to a deeper understanding of ourselves and the Divine. By cultivating love and compassion, we align ourselves with the nature of God and foster a spiritual journey that is rich, meaningful, and transformative.

Chapter 5: The Divine Within

The concept of divinity dwelling within each individual is a profound and transformative idea that resonates across spiritual traditions. This idea invites us to explore the depths of our being and reveals that the essence of God is not a distant entity, but an intrinsic part of our existence. Recognizing this divine presence within ourselves is not merely an abstract philosophical exercise; it is a journey of self-awareness that can lead to profound personal transformation and a deeper connection with the universe.

At the heart of this exploration is the understanding that each person is a unique manifestation of the Divine. This perspective shifts the focus from seeking God externally to recognizing that the divine spark resides within us. It challenges us to look within, to confront our fears, insecurities, and limitations, and to embrace the fullness of our humanity. The journey within is often fraught with challenges as it requires us to peel back the layers of conditioning and societal expectations that obscure our true nature. However, it is through this process of self-discovery that we can begin to understand our purpose and the role we play in the grand tapestry of existence.

Self-knowledge is the key to unlocking the divine potential within. It is the ability to observe our thoughts, emotions, and actions without judgment, allowing us to gain insight into our true selves. This practice of introspection fosters a deeper understanding of our motivations and desires, enabling us to align our actions with our higher purpose. As we cultivate self-awareness, we begin to recognize the interconnectedness of all beings and the divine energy that flows through us. This realization can be both liberating and humbling, reminding us that we are part of something much greater than ourselves.

The teachings of various spiritual traditions emphasize the importance of self-awareness in recognizing the divine within. For example, many Eastern philosophies advocate meditation as a tool for cultivating inner awareness. This practice encourages us to quiet the mind and connect with our inner self, allowing us to experience the divine presence that resides within. Similarly, Western spiritual traditions often emphasize the importance of prayer and reflection as a means of fostering a deeper connection with God. In both cases, the underlying message is clear: the path to understanding the divine begins with an exploration of the self.

As we embark on this journey of self-discovery, we may encounter resistance from within. The ego, with its need for validation and control, often seeks to maintain the status quo, fearing the changes that self-knowledge may bring. This internal struggle may manifest as self-doubt, fear of failure, or an unwillingness to face uncomfortable truths. However, it is important to recognize that these challenges are part of the process. Embracing vulnerability and allowing ourselves to be open to change is crucial to spiritual growth. By surrendering to the journey and trusting in the process, we can transcend the limitations imposed by the ego and connect with our true essence.

The divine within us is not a static entity; it is a dynamic force that evolves as we grow and change. Every experience we have, whether joyful or painful, contributes to our understanding of ourselves and our relationship with the Divine. This perspective encourages us to see challenges as opportunities for growth rather than obstacles to be avoided. By reframing our experiences in this way, we can cultivate resilience and a deeper appreciation for life's journey.

In addition, recognizing the divine within ourselves has profound implications for how we relate to others. When we acknowledge our own divinity, we are more likely to see the divine in others. This shift in perspective fosters compassion, empathy, and understanding, allowing us to connect with others on a deeper level. It reminds us that we are all part of the same universal fabric, each contributing our unique threads to the tapestry of existence.

Chapter 6: God and the Universe

The relationship between God and the cosmos is a profound inquiry that has captivated the minds of philosophers, theologians, and scientists alike. This inquiry invites us to see the universe not merely as a vast expanse of matter and energy, but as a living expression of divine will. Understanding creation in this light allows us to appreciate the intricate tapestry of existence in which every thread is woven with purpose and intention, reflecting the nature of the Creator.

At the heart of this relationship is the concept of God as the ultimate source of all that exists. In many spiritual traditions, God is seen as the architect of the universe, the force that brings order out of chaos and gives meaning to life. This perspective challenges us to see the cosmos as a manifestation of divine creativity, where each star, planet, and living being is imbued with a unique essence that contributes to the whole. In this sense, the universe is not a random collection of particles, but a harmonious symphony orchestrated by a higher intelligence.

Creation, as an expression of divine will, invites us to reflect on the purpose of our existence. If we accept that the universe is a deliberate act of creation, we must also consider the implications of this belief for our understanding of life and our place within it. Each individual is not merely a byproduct of chance, but an essential part of the cosmic design. This realization fosters a sense of responsibility and urges us to engage with the world around us in a way that honors the divine intention behind our creation.

The teachings of various spiritual traditions emphasize the interconnectedness of all beings within the cosmos. This interconnectedness is often described as a web of life, where every action reverberates through the fabric of existence. In this view, the universe is a living organism, and we are its conscious participants. Our thoughts, emotions, and actions contribute to the overall energy of the cosmos and shape the reality we experience. This understanding is consistent with the principle that we are co-creators with God, actively participating in the unfolding of the universe.

In addition, the relationship between God and the universe invites us to explore the nature of divine will. Many spiritual teachings suggest that God's will is not a rigid blueprint that dictates every detail of existence, but rather a dynamic force that allows for free will and creativity. This perspective encourages us to embrace the uncertainties of life, recognizing that challenges and obstacles are not mere accidents, but opportunities for growth and transformation. In this light, the universe becomes a sacred space for learning, where every experience serves as a lesson in the grand design of creation.

The cosmos also reflects the duality of existence, embodying both light and darkness, creation and destruction. This duality is essential to understanding the nature of God, who encompasses all aspects of existence. The interplay of these forces creates a balance that sustains the universe and reminds us that both joy and suffering are integral to the human experience. By embracing this duality, we can cultivate a deeper understanding of our own lives, recognizing that every challenge holds the potential for growth and every moment of joy is a glimpse of the divine.

As we contemplate the relationship between God and the universe, we are also led to consider the role of consciousness in this dynamic. Consciousness is often seen as the bridge between the divine and the material world, allowing us to perceive and interact with the cosmos. This perspective suggests that our consciousness is not separate from the universe, but is in fact a reflection of the divine consciousness that pervades all existence. By expanding our awareness, we can deepen our connection to the cosmos and experience the divine presence in every aspect of life.

Chapter 7: The Illusion of Separation

The belief in separation from God is one of humanity's most entrenched illusions, influencing our perceptions, beliefs, and interactions with the world. This illusion fosters a sense of isolation, causing us to feel disconnected from the divine source that sustains all life. However, this separation is not a fundamental reality, but a mental construct - a veil that obscures the truth of our oneness with the Divine. Recognizing this illusion is the first step toward awakening to the profound interconnectedness that binds us to God and to each other.

At the heart of this illusion is the ego, a construct that thrives on the perception of individuality and separation. The ego creates a false narrative that portrays us as isolated beings, separate from the universe and the divine. This narrative is reinforced by societal norms, cultural beliefs, and personal experiences that emphasize competition, comparison, and individual achievement. As we navigate life, the ego often leads us to prioritize external validation and material success over spiritual fulfillment and inner peace, perpetuating the illusion of separation and causing us to overlook the inherent unity within creation.

To transcend this illusion, we must cultivate a deeper awareness of our consciousness. Consciousness is the bridge that connects us to the Divine and allows us to perceive the interconnectedness of all beings. Through awareness, we can recognize the divine presence within ourselves and others. This recognition is not merely intellectual; it is an experiential realization that transforms our perception of reality.

The journey to oneness with the Divine requires a commitment to self-exploration and introspection. It involves examining and shedding the layers of conditioning and societal expectations that have shaped our beliefs about ourselves and our relationship with God. By facing these challenges, we can dismantle the barriers that prevent us from experiencing our true nature as expressions of the Divine.

Meditation and contemplative practices are powerful tools for cultivating awareness and fostering a sense of oneness with the Divine. These practices encourage us to quiet the mind, turn inward, and connect with the deeper aspects of our being. In moments of stillness, we can access the profound wisdom that resides within us, allowing us to transcend the illusion of separation and experience the divine presence that is always available. As we deepen our connection to our inner self, we realize that the Divine is not an external entity to be sought, but an intrinsic part of our existence.

Furthermore, realizing our oneness with the Divine has profound implications for how we relate to others. When we recognize that we are all interconnected expressions of the same Divine Source, our interactions with others change dramatically. We begin to see beyond the superficial differences that often divide us-such as race, religion, and socioeconomic status-and focus instead on the common humanity that binds us together. This shift in perspective fosters compassion, empathy, and understanding, allowing us to build bridges of connection rather than walls of separation.

Various spiritual traditions teach the importance of love and compassion as pathways to unity with the Divine. Love is the highest expression of consciousness that transcends the limitations of the ego and dissolves the illusion of separation. When we approach life from a place of love, we align ourselves with the divine will and experience the fullness of our connection to God and to each other. This love is not limited to romantic or family relationships; it extends to all beings and invites us to embrace the inherent divinity in everyone we encounter.

Chapter 8: God and Suffering

The complex relationship between suffering and spiritual growth is a profound aspect of the human experience that often puzzles us. Many struggle with the question of why suffering exists, especially when considering the concept of a benevolent God. Exploring the nature of suffering, however, reveals its vital role as a catalyst for personal transformation. By understanding pain as a pathway to enlightenment, we can reframe our experiences, seeing them not only as hardships, but as opportunities for growth and deeper connection with the Divine.

Suffering is an intrinsic part of the human condition, manifesting in various forms such as physical pain, emotional distress, and existential crisis. While it is natural to want to avoid suffering, it is important to recognize that pain often serves a higher purpose. It can act as a teacher, leading us to self-discovery and deeper understanding. In moments of suffering, we are often stripped of our illusions and forced to confront the realities of our existence. This confrontation can lead to profound insights about ourselves, our relationships, and our connection to the Divine.

It is to be expected that as you improve spiritually, many of your associations with people of a lower spiritual nature will begin to dissolve. Either through unexplained circumstances, an illogical hatred of your presence that causes them to push you away, or positive but unimaginable opportunities, you see a great shift in your reality that pulls you from one scenario to another. However, because people refuse to accept suffering and instead run away from it, they constantly miss the greatest opportunities that come their way. In fact, many will never develop the ability to see such things, even though the lives of successful people constantly show that you must overcome adversity and hopelessness before you can discover the spiritual journey you are being asked to take.

The things that depress and sadden you the most are the very things you must let go of in order to find better experiences in your life. Often this means breaking the bond with your family if they have never supported you in your dreams and deep in their soul wish you to fail. There is no other way but to let them die within you before you can be reborn as the person you were meant to be. Those who are emotionally dependent on the approval of family members will never understand how to find their true selves.

Many spiritual traditions emphasize the transformative power of suffering. Many Eastern philosophies, for example, view suffering as an integral part of the path to enlightenment. The Buddha taught that life involves suffering, and it is through acknowledging and understanding this suffering that one can attain liberation. This perspective encourages individuals to accept their pain not as a permanent condition, but as a necessary step on the path to spiritual awakening.

In addition, suffering can shake us out of complacency and into action, prompting us to reevaluate our priorities and values. During times of pain, we may find ourselves questioning our beliefs, relationships, and life choices. This introspection can lead to significant personal growth as we learn to let go of what no longer serves us and embrace new possibilities. The process of transformation often requires us to confront our fears and insecurities, allowing us to emerge stronger and more aligned with our true selves.

Understanding pain as a path to enlightenment also invites us to cultivate gratitude for our experiences, even the challenging ones. When we shift our perspective to see suffering as a teacher, we can begin to appreciate the lessons it offers. Each moment of pain holds the potential for growth, urging us to expand our awareness and deepen our connection to the divine. This shift in attitude can be liberating, enabling us to face life's challenges with confidence.

In addition, the experience of suffering can foster empathy and compassion for others. When we endure pain, we gain a deeper understanding of the struggles of those around us. This shared experience of suffering can create a sense of unity, reminding us that we are all interconnected in our humanity. When we cultivate compassion for ourselves, we naturally extend that compassion to others, creating a ripple effect of healing and understanding in the world.

In the context of spiritual growth, suffering can also serve as a powerful motivator to seek a deeper connection with God. In times of need, many people turn to prayer, meditation, or other spiritual practices for comfort and guidance. This search for connection can lead to profound moments of insight and revelation as we open ourselves to the divine presence that permeates all aspects of life. Through suffering, we may come to realize that we are never truly alone; the Divine is always present, offering support and love even in our darkest moments.

Chapter 9: The Power of Prayer

Prayer is a profound and multifaceted practice that serves as a bridge between the human mind and the Divine. It is a means of connecting with God and expressing our innermost thoughts, desires, and fears. The significance of prayer transcends mere ritual; it is a vital component of spiritual life that fosters a deeper understanding of ourselves and our place in the universe. Through prayer, we engage in a dialogue with the divine, seeking guidance, comfort, and strength in our daily lives.

The act of prayer can take many forms, each with its own unique impact on our spiritual journey. Traditional prayers, often recited in community, create a sense of belonging and unity among participants. These collective expressions of faith reinforce the idea that we are part of something greater than ourselves, a community bound by shared beliefs and values. In contrast, personal prayer, which can be spontaneous or structured, allows for intimate conversations with God. This personal connection can be incredibly transformative, encouraging vulnerability and honesty in our relationship with the divine.

One of the most powerful aspects of prayer is its ability to cultivate presence. When we pray, we often find ourselves in a state of reflection, contemplating our lives, our choices, and our desires. This introspection can lead to greater self-awareness, helping us to identify areas in our lives that need change or improvement. As we engage in this process, we may find that our prayers evolve, reflecting our growth and changing perspectives. This dynamic nature of prayer underscores its role as a living practice that adapts to our changing circumstances and spiritual needs.

In addition, prayer serves as a source of comfort in times of need. In moments of uncertainty or despair, turning to prayer can provide solace and reassurance. It is in these vulnerable moments that we often feel most connected to the divine as we seek guidance and support. The act of surrendering our worries and fears to God can be liberating, allowing us to release the burdens we carry and trust in a higher plan. This sense of surrender is not a sign of weakness; rather, it is an acknowledgment of our limitations and a recognition of the strength that comes from faith.

The effect of prayer goes beyond the individual; it can also affect our relationships with others. When we pray for others, we cultivate empathy and compassion, recognizing the common human experience of suffering and joy. This practice fosters a sense of connectedness and reminds us that we are not alone in our struggles. By keeping others in our thoughts and prayers, we contribute to a collective energy of healing and support that can have a ripple effect in our communities.

In addition to its emotional and relational benefits, prayer can serve as a catalyst for personal transformation. As we engage in prayer, we may find ourselves inspired to take action in our lives, whether that means making amends, embarking on a new path, or deepening our commitment to our spiritual practice. This alignment of intention and action is crucial to personal growth, as it allows us to manifest the changes we seek in our lives. The insights gained through prayer can illuminate our paths and guide us toward choices that resonate with our true selves.

In addition, the practice of gratitude in prayer cannot be overlooked. Expressing gratitude for the blessings in our lives shifts our focus from what we lack to what we have. This shift in perspective can lead to a more positive outlook that enhances our overall well-being. When we acknowledge the abundance in our lives, we cultivate a sense of contentment and joy that can sustain us through challenging times.

As we explore the various dimensions of prayer, it becomes clear that its power lies not only in the act itself, but also in the intention behind it. Whether we approach prayer with a sense of urgency, seeking immediate answers, or with a spirit of openness, allowing for divine timing, our intentions shape our experience. The sincerity of our prayers, coupled with our willingness to listen and be receptive, can open doors to profound insights and revelations.

Chapter 10: God and Morality

The interplay between faith and morality raises fundamental questions about the nature of good and evil, the role of divine commandments, and the human capacity for moral reasoning. At their core, the moral implications of divine teachings are rooted in the belief that God embodies the ultimate standard of goodness.

Many religious traditions assert that moral laws are not merely human constructs, but are divinely ordained. From this perspective, an understanding of God's nature-characterized by love, justice, and mercy-provides a framework for discerning right from wrong. In Christianity, for example, the teachings of Jesus emphasize love and compassion as central tenets of moral behavior. The commandment to "love thy neighbor as thyself" encapsulates a moral directive that transcends cultural and temporal boundaries, urging individuals to act with empathy and kindness toward others.

In addition, the moral teachings attributed to God often serve as a guide for ethical behavior and shape the conscience of believers.

These teachings can be thought of as a moral compass, pointing individuals toward actions that are consistent with the divine will. For example, the Ten Commandments in the Judeo-Christian tradition outline fundamental ethical principles that govern human behavior, such as prohibitions against theft, murder, and false witness. These commandments not only establish societal norms, but also reflect a deeper moral order that believers are encouraged to uphold. The understanding that these laws come from a divine source gives them a sense of authority and importance that compels adherents to internalize and practice them in their daily lives.

The relationship between God and morality, however, is not without its complexities. One major challenge is the question of moral autonomy. If moral laws are perceived as divinely mandated, does this imply that individuals are merely following orders rather than exercising their moral agency? This dilemma raises critical discussions about the nature of free will and the capacity for moral reasoning. Many theologians argue that true morality involves a conscious decision to align one's actions with divine teachings, suggesting that an understanding of God enhances rather than diminishes moral agency. In this view, individuals are called to actively engage their faith by reflecting on how divine principles apply to their unique circumstances and choices.

Moreover, the influence of an understanding of God on ethical behavior goes beyond mere compliance with rules. It fosters a transformative relationship that encourages individuals to cultivate virtues such as humility, integrity, and compassion. When believers perceive God as a loving and just being, they are more likely to embody these qualities in their interactions with others. This relational aspect of faith emphasizes that morality is not just about following commandments, but also about cultivating a character that reflects divine attributes. The teachings of various religious traditions often emphasize the importance of inner transformation, suggesting that a genuine understanding of God leads to a profound change in the way individuals relate to themselves and others.

In addition, the moral implications of divine teachings can be seen in the context of social justice and ethical responsibility. Many religious traditions advocate for the marginalized and oppressed and encourage believers to promote justice and equity. This call to action is often rooted in the belief that God's concern extends to all of creation, and that ethical behavior includes speaking out against injustice and defending those who have no voice. Understanding God as a defender of justice leads people to become involved in social issues and fosters a sense of moral obligation to make a positive contribution to society.

In fact, several studies of the effects of ethical actions on the individual who practices them suggest that ethical and authentic behavior promotes feelings of well-being and increases neurological capacity. For example, a study by Dunn, Aknin, and Norton (2008) found that spending money on others (an ethical behavior) increased personal happiness more than spending money on oneself. On the other hand, a study by Shu, Gino, and Bazerman (2011) found that people who engage in unethical behavior tend to justify their actions in order to maintain a positive self-image. However, this can lead to an increase in cognitive dissonance and psychological distress.

Chapter 11: The Pursuit of Truth

The pursuit of truth is a profound spiritual journey that transcends mere intellectual curiosity. It is a deeply transformative process that shapes our understanding of ourselves, our relationships, and ultimately our connection to the Divine. In a world filled with distractions, misinformation, and competing narratives, the search for truth serves as a guiding light that leads us to a deeper understanding of God and our place in the universe. At the heart of this quest is the recognition that truth is not a static concept, but a dynamic, evolving understanding. It is shaped by our experiences, beliefs, and the insights we gain along the way.

As we embark on this journey, we often encounter different layers of truth, each revealing a different aspect of reality. The early stages may involve confronting uncomfortable truths about ourselves-our fears, biases, and limitations. This self-examination is crucial because it lays the foundation for a deeper understanding of the world around us. The process of peeling back these layers can be challenging, but it is essential for spiritual growth.

In many spiritual traditions, the search for truth is intertwined with the concept of self-knowledge. As we become more attuned to our inner selves, we begin to recognize the illusions that cloud our perception. The teachings of various sages emphasize that ignorance is often the greatest obstacle to enlightenment. For example, the idea that what the conscience does not recognize, the eyes cannot see encapsulates the notion that our understanding of truth is limited by our level of awareness. This realization compels us to engage in an ongoing process of introspection and reflection, and encourages us to confront the shadows within us that obscure our vision.

Moreover, the search for truth is not only an individual endeavor; it is also a collective journey. Throughout history, communities have come together to seek truth, often through shared rituals, discussions, and explorations of sacred texts. These communal practices serve to reinforce the idea that truth is not merely a personal revelation, but a universal principle that binds humanity together. The insights gained from collective experience can illuminate paths that individuals might not have discovered on their own. This interconnectedness underscores the importance of humility in our search, recognizing that our understanding is enriched by the perspectives of others.

As we delve deeper into the search for truth, we inevitably encounter the divine. The relationship between truth and God is profound, for many spiritual teachings assert that God embodies ultimate truth. This connection invites us to explore how our understanding of truth influences our perception of the Divine. When we approach God with an open heart and a sincere desire to understand, we often find that our experiences of the divine become more vibrant and transformative. The teachings of various religious traditions emphasize that truth leads to a deeper relationship with God because it fosters a sense of trust and faith in the divine plan.

In this context, the pursuit of truth can be seen as a path to spiritual awakening. When we align ourselves with truth, we begin to resonate with the frequencies of love and understanding that characterize the divine nature. This alignment not only enhances our spiritual life, but also influences our ethical behavior. When we act in accordance with truth, we cultivate virtues that reflect the divine qualities we seek to embody. The teachings of many spiritual leaders remind us that our actions should be guided by a commitment to truth, for this commitment ultimately leads to a more harmonious existence.

However, the world is full of distractions and falsehoods that can easily lead us astray. The temptation to accept convenient truths or to conform to societal norms can hinder our progress. It is essential to cultivate discernment, the ability to distinguish between what resonates with our inner truth and what is merely a reflection of external influences. This discernment is a skill that can be developed through practices such as meditation, contemplation, and critical thinking. By honing our ability to discern, we empower ourselves to navigate the complexities of life with clarity and purpose.

Chapter 12: God and Human Potential

Recognizing God is often seen as a transformative experience that unlocks the vast potential within each individual. This profound realization serves as a catalyst for personal growth, enabling people to transcend their limitations and achieve greatness. The relationship between spirituality and human potential is complex, interwoven with threads of faith, self-awareness, and the pursuit of higher ideals. By understanding and embracing the divine, individuals can tap into a reservoir of strength and creativity that propels them toward their aspirations.

At the heart of this exploration is the understanding that acknowledging God is more than an act of faith; it is a profound awakening to the interconnectedness of all existence. This awareness fosters a sense of purpose and belonging as individuals realize they are part of a larger cosmic design. Various spiritual traditions teach that each person is endowed with unique gifts and talents that often lie dormant until awakened through the recognition of the divine. This awakening is akin to lighting a flame within that illuminates the path to self-discovery and fulfillment.

The journey to unlocking human potential begins with self-knowledge. As individuals recognize the divine presence within themselves, they are encouraged to reflect on their values, desires, and aspirations. This introspective process allows them to confront their fears and limitations, ultimately leading to a deeper understanding of their true selves. The starting point for true knowledge is self-awareness. We only become aware of the reality of a subject when we can feel it. Thus, there is a need to cultivate emotional intelligence in the pursuit of personal growth.

In addition, spirituality serves as a powerful motivator that empowers individuals to pursue their dreams with unwavering determination. When one recognizes God as a source of strength and inspiration, challenges that once seemed insurmountable become opportunities for growth. The belief in divine support fosters resilience, enabling individuals to overcome obstacles with perseverance. In fact, the more happiness we feel, the more energy we have to push ourselves toward the desired goal. This link between spirituality and motivation highlights the transformative power of faith in the pursuit of greatness.

In addition to fostering resilience, spirituality cultivates a sense of responsibility to self and others. The knowledge of God provides a moral compass that guides individuals in their actions and decisions. This ethical framework encourages individuals to act with integrity, compassion, and empathy, ultimately contributing to the greater good. Spiritual leaders emphasize that true greatness is measured not only by personal accomplishments, but also by the positive impact one has on the lives of others. This perspective is consistent with the idea that human potential is maximized when individuals work together toward common goals, fostering a sense of community and interconnectedness.

In addition, the recognition of God can lead to a profound shift in perspective, allowing individuals to see beyond their immediate circumstances. This broader view enables them to see challenges as opportunities for growth and transformation. The purpose of reality is to foster the development of understanding through knowledge of the cause-and-effect laws that govern that same reality. This understanding empowers individuals to take responsibility for their experiences by recognizing that their thoughts and actions shape their reality. By aligning their intentions with divine principles, they can manifest their desires and aspirations.

The journey to unlocking human potential is also marked by the cultivation of creativity. As individuals recognize the divine spark within themselves, they are inspired to express their unique gifts in innovative ways. This creative expression is not limited to the arts; it encompasses all aspects of life, including problem solving, leadership, and personal relationships. Spiritual teachings encourage individuals to embrace their creativity as a reflection of the divine, fostering a sense of joy and fulfillment in the process. The more we dream, the more we increase our life energy. This connection between creativity and spiritual awareness underscores the importance of nurturing one's imagination in the pursuit of greatness.

Chapter 13: The Nature of Evil

Understanding the nature of evil is a complex and often disturbing endeavor, especially when viewed through the lens of divine creation. The existence of evil raises profound questions about the nature of God, the purpose of life, and the role of human agency. To address these questions, one must consider the complex interplay between divine purpose and human free will, and the implications of these concepts for our understanding of morality and existence.

At its core, evil can be seen as a deviation from the divine order established by God. Many religious traditions assert that God is inherently good, which makes the existence of evil a paradox. If God is omnipotent and omnipresent, how can evil exist in the world? This question has puzzled theologians and philosophers for centuries, leading to various interpretations and explanations. One common view is that evil is not a direct creation of God, but rather a consequence of human free will. This perspective suggests that God has given humanity the gift of free will, allowing individuals to make choices that can lead to both good and evil outcomes.

The role of free will in the existence of evil is crucial to understanding the nature of evil. Free will is often seen as a fundamental aspect of what it means to be human. It allows individuals to choose their paths, to act with intention, and to experience the consequences of their actions. With this freedom, however, comes the potential for moral failure. When individuals exercise their free will in ways that harm others or themselves, they contribute to the manifestation of evil in the world. Every choice we make is an encounter with destiny. Each choice therefore carries weight and significance, shaping not only individual lives but also the broader tapestry of human experience.

Moreover, the existence of evil can be seen as a necessary counterpart to the concept of good. In a world of free will, the potential for evil is an inherent aspect of the human condition. Without the possibility of choosing evil, the concept of good would lose its meaning. This duality is reflected in the teachings of various spiritual traditions, which often emphasize the importance of moral discernment and the cultivation of virtues. The struggle between good and evil is not only external, but also internal, as individuals grapple with their desires, fears, and moral convictions.

The recognition of evil as a product of free will also invites a deeper exploration of personal responsibility. When individuals acknowledge their capacity to choose, they are forced to confront the consequences of their actions. This awareness fosters a sense of accountability that compels individuals to reflect on their choices and their impact on others. Ultimately, positive choices can lead to constructive outcomes, while negative choices can perpetuate cycles of harm and suffering.

Furthermore, understanding evil in the context of divine creation invites consideration of the nature of suffering. Many spiritual traditions assert that suffering can serve a purpose, acting as a catalyst for growth and transformation. In this view, the experience of evil and suffering can lead individuals to seek deeper truths and foster empathy, wisdom, and solitude. The trials and tribulations of life can cause individuals to reflect on their values and priorities, ultimately leading them to a deeper understanding of themselves and their relationship to the divine.

However, the existence of evil also raises challenging questions about the nature of divine justice and mercy. If God is omnipotent and omnipresent, why does evil persist? This question often leads to discussions about the nature of divine intervention and the limits of human understanding. Some theologians argue that God's ways are beyond human comprehension and suggest that the existence of evil may serve a greater purpose, even if it is not immediately apparent. This perspective encourages people to cultivate faith and trust in the divine plan, even in the face of suffering and injustice.

The truth is that without the evil provided by free will, it would not be possible to distinguish the good souls from those who do not deserve a more meaningful eternal life. In this context, the divine plan would not matter. This doesn't mean that we should tolerate people with negative intentions, but that we should persevere in spite of their existence and unethical behavior, because only in this way do we manifest the divine purpose in ourselves and in the world.

Chapter 14: God and Community

In a world that often emphasizes individualism, the role of community in spiritual growth and development cannot be overstated. Communities serve as fertile ground where faith is nurtured, convictions are strengthened, and people are empowered to explore their spirituality in a mutually supportive environment. The need for connection and belonging is deeply rooted in our nature and extends to our spiritual lives. Communities provide a space where people can come together to share beliefs, experiences, and aspirations. This collective engagement fosters a sense of unity and support that makes people feel supported in their spiritual endeavors. Everyone we meet in life brings us closer to what we need. Therefore, our interactions within a community can guide us along our spiritual paths and enrich our understanding of God and ourselves.

In addition, the community aspect of spirituality often leads to the creation of rituals and practices that reinforce shared beliefs. These rituals are powerful expressions of faith that allow people to connect collectively with the divine. Whether through prayer, meditation, or communal worship, these practices create a sense of shared purpose and intention. They remind us that we are not alone in our spiritual journeys, but part of a larger web of faith that transcends individual experiences. The collective energy generated during these gatherings can expand the spiritual experience and create deep connections with God and others.

The importance of community in spiritual practice extends to the concept of shared responsibility. When people embrace a shared belief system, they often take responsibility for each other's actions and choices. This accountability fosters a sense of ownership that encourages people to align their behavior with their spiritual values. In this context, community acts as a mirror, reflecting our strengths and weaknesses. It challenges us to grow and evolve, leading us to face our limitations and seek a broader understanding.

In addition, the collective faith of the community significantly shapes our understanding of God. Different communities may interpret the divine through different lenses, influenced by cultural, historical, and social contexts. This diversity of perspectives enriches our understanding of God and allows us to explore the multifaceted nature of the divine. Exposure to different beliefs and practices can challenge our preconceived notions and broaden our spiritual horizons. As we encounter different interpretations of God, we are invited to reflect on our beliefs and consider how they fit into the broader human experience.

The community aspect of spirituality is also fundamental in addressing the challenges and struggles people face. In times of crisis or difficulty, the support of a community can provide comfort and strength. Shared experiences of suffering and joy create bonds that transcend individual struggles and foster empathy and compassion. This collective support can be transformative, enabling people to face their challenges with hope and resilience. We should expect change for better or worse, but we should always focus on feeling good about ourselves, because even negative change can lead to better life experiences. In this way, community can play an important role in maintaining a positive outlook even in the face of adversity.

In addition, the role of community in spiritual practice extends beyond the individual to include social responsibility. Many spiritual traditions emphasize the importance of serving others and contributing to the common good. Communities often mobilize to address social issues and advocate for justice, compassion, and equality. This collective action reflects a shared understanding of God as a force for good in the world, inspiring people to work together to bring about positive change. The teachings of various spiritual leaders remind us that our understanding of God is intimately connected to our actions in the world. By engaging in acts of service and compassion, we embody the divine qualities we seek to understand. It is through selfless acts that the divine expression finds its way into our hearts and teaches us valuable lessons about ourselves and the world around us. These lessons transform the potential of our destiny, changing it from a state of predictability to one of unpredictability.

Through altruistic acts, we influence the structure of our reality, expanding infinite possibilities and creating states of unpredictable receptivity in which miracles change our destiny. In fact, these books were born out of a personal transformation, as the act of helping children with learning disabilities radically altered my approach to knowledge and allowed me to visualize new ways of interacting with the world. My experience as a college lecturer, which led me to answer existential questions unrelated to my teaching, added a new understanding and empathy that built bridges between the knowledge I acquired and the existential needs of others. Finally, helping many people achieve their financial goals has allowed me to see personal and financial fulfillment from a new, more holistic and spiritual perspective, which has indeed changed my self-image and transformed me from a simple teacher into a wealthy writer who travels the world.

Chapter 15: The Transformative Power of Love

Love, the highest expression of the divine, is a force that transcends the ordinary and connects us to the essence of existence. More than an emotion, it is a profound state of being capable of transforming lives and communities. The teachings of love emphasize that it serves as the foundation for all meaningful relationships and guides our interactions with others.

At its core, love embodies empathy, compassion, and understanding. It encourages us to look beyond our own needs and desires and to recognize the interconnectedness of all beings. This recognition fosters a sense of oneness and reminds us that we are not isolated, but part of a larger tapestry of life. When we embrace love, we open ourselves to profound change-both within ourselves and in the world around us.

The transformative power of love is evident in its ability to heal wounds, both personal and collective. Acting as a balm for the soul, love eases the pain of past traumas and offers a path to forgiveness and reconciliation. It encourages us to face our fears and insecurities, allowing us to emerge stronger and more resilient. In this way, love becomes a catalyst for personal growth, pushing us to evolve beyond our limitations and embrace our true potential.

In addition, love has the ability to inspire action. When we are motivated by love, we are compelled to serve others, to lift up those who are struggling, and to work for justice and equality. This sense of purpose can ignite movements that challenge societal norms and bring about significant change. History is filled with examples of individuals and communities who have harnessed the power of love to effect positive change, from civil rights activists to humanitarian efforts to alleviate suffering.

In communities where love is a priority, creativity, cooperation, and mutual support flourish. Love fosters an environment where individuals feel safe to express themselves, share their ideas, and work together toward common goals. This collective spirit not only enhances the quality of life for all members, but also cultivates a sense of belonging and purpose. When love permeates a community, it creates a ripple effect that inspires others to engage in acts of kindness and compassion.

The journey of love, however, is not without challenges. It requires vulnerability and a willingness to face our own shadows. Love requires that we acknowledge our fears, biases, and prejudices and work to transcend them. This process can be uncomfortable because it often involves confronting the parts of ourselves that we would rather ignore. Yet it is through this discomfort that we can experience the most profound growth.

The teachings of love also remind us that it is not a finite resource, but rather an infinite source that can be cultivated and shared. The more we give love, the more we receive in return. This reciprocal nature of love reinforces the idea that our actions have consequences, and that by cultivating love within ourselves, we contribute to a more compassionate world.

In a society that often prioritizes individualism and competition, the call to love can feel revolutionary. It challenges us to shift our focus from self-interest to the well-being of others. This shift is essential to creating a sustainable future because it encourages us to consider the impact of our choices on the planet and on future generations. Love compels us to act with integrity and responsibility, recognizing that our interconnectedness extends beyond human relationships to include all living beings and the environment.

Love is not just an ideal to aspire to, but a practical tool for creating meaningful change. By embodying love in our thoughts, words, and actions, we can contribute to a more just, equitable, and harmonious world.

Chapter 16: Life After Death

The concept of life after death has been a fundamental aspect of human spirituality and belief systems throughout history. It encompasses a wide range of beliefs about what happens after death, often tied to notions of divine judgment and moral accountability. Exploring these beliefs offers insights into the human condition and reveals the profound implications of the afterlife for spiritual practice and ethical living. The relationship between God and the afterlife invites us to reflect on our actions, our values, and the legacy we leave behind.

At the core of many religious traditions is a belief in an afterlife, a continuation of existence beyond the physical realm. This belief is often comforting, providing individuals with hope and a sense of purpose. Various faiths teach that life on earth is a preparation for what lies beyond, a realm where our choices and actions determine our destiny. This perspective is consistent with the idea that our pursuit of spiritual growth and ethical living is paramount, as we strive to align our lives with divine principles in anticipation of the judgment that awaits us.

Divine judgment is a central theme in discussions of the afterlife. Many religious traditions assert that individuals will be held accountable for their actions during their earthly lives. This notion of judgment serves as a moral compass, guiding individuals to consider the consequences of their choices. The fear of divine retribution can deter immoral behavior, while the promise of reward for a virtuous life can inspire individuals to strive for goodness. The ultimate test comes in the form of that which is most desired, hidden beneath the layer of that which is simultaneously feared. This duality highlights the internal struggle individuals face as they navigate their moral landscapes, balancing their desires with the ethical implications of their actions.

The implications of life after death go beyond individual accountability; they also shape communal values and social norms. When a community collectively believes in an afterlife, it fosters a shared understanding of morality and ethics. This shared belief can create a sense of unity as individuals come together to uphold shared values and support one another on their spiritual journeys. Spiritual leaders emphasize the importance of community in this context, as collective belief can amplify the impact of individual actions. The idea that we draw people into our lives with our souls, keep them with our hearts, and push them away with our minds underscores the interconnectedness of human relationships and the role of shared beliefs in shaping our experiences.

In addition, belief in an afterlife can profoundly influence spiritual practices. Many religious traditions include rituals and practices designed to honor the deceased and facilitate their journey in the afterlife. These practices serve as a means of expressing love and respect for the deceased and reinforce the idea that life continues after death. Rituals such as prayer, meditation, and offerings can create a sense of connection between the living and the deceased, fostering a deeper understanding of the cyclical nature of existence.

The implications of life after death also extend to how individuals approach their daily lives. The awareness that our actions have eternal consequences can inspire a sense of urgency in the pursuit of spiritual growth and ethical living. This perspective encourages individuals to reflect on their values and priorities and to live with intention and purpose. Spiritual traditions emphasize the importance of living in alignment with one's beliefs, as this alignment can lead to a more fulfilling and meaningful existence. The realization that the answers to everything we ever wanted have always been within us serves as a reminder that the journey to understanding life after death begins with self-exploration and introspection.

However, fear of judgment and the unknown can lead to anxiety and existential angst. Individuals may struggle with questions about their worthiness and the nature of divine judgment, leading to feelings of guilt and shame. It is important to approach these beliefs with a sense of balance, recognizing that while accountability is important, so is an understanding of divine love and mercy. Many spiritual traditions emphasize that the divine is not only a judge, but also a source of compassion and forgiveness. This understanding can alleviate the burdens of fear and guilt, allowing individuals to approach their spiritual journeys with a sense of hope and possibility.

Indeed, nothing better expresses divine mercy than death as a transitory process of unlimited learning and reincarnation as an opportunity to begin again. It is through spiritual life without a body that the individual acquires a timeless and unlimited awareness of all his failures. It is through this awareness that a genuine need for divine forgiveness develops. And it is also through this awareness that the spirit chooses to reincarnate in a context full of financial and even physical difficulties in order to force itself onto a path of reflection and improvement in its role as an immortal spirit capable of influencing the destiny of others.

However, reincarnation can be a wasted opportunity if we are reborn as the parents of those who were our grandparents, or of people we harmed in other lives and failed to love and support the beings in our care. Similarly, we must consider that all the people we meet along the way may have been others in past lives whom we need to help to make up for past mistakes. No one fails so drastically in this regard as the racist, the xenophobe, the arrogant, the presumptuous, the chauvinist, the ethnocentric, the jingoist, or the bigot. These states of mind represent the worst among us.

Chapter 17: The Language of God

Exploring the language of God reveals a profound interplay between symbols, metaphors, and the spiritual texts that attempt to convey the divine essence. Language, in its various forms, serves as a bridge between human experience and the transcendent realities that lie beyond our immediate perception. Understanding the symbols and metaphors embedded in spiritual texts not only enriches our understanding of the divine, but also shapes our perception of God and our relationship with the sacred.

At the heart of spiritual texts is a rich tapestry of symbols and metaphors that convey complex truths about existence, morality, and the nature of God. These linguistic devices serve as tools for expressing the ineffable, allowing authors to articulate experiences and insights that transcend ordinary language. The answers to everything we have ever wanted have always been within us. The divine is not external, but an intrinsic part of our being, waiting to be discovered through the exploration of language and meaning.

Symbols play an important role in spiritual texts. They encapsulate profound concepts and ideas, often drawn from cultural and historical contexts that resonate with the reader. For example, the use of light as a symbol of knowledge and enlightenment is prevalent in various spiritual traditions. This metaphor not only conveys the idea of illumination, but also suggests a journey from darkness to understanding. The language of symbols invites the individual to engage with the text on a deeper level, encouraging reflection and introspection. As we decipher these symbols, we uncover layers of meaning that enrich our spiritual journeys and deepen our connection to the Divine.

In addition, metaphors serve as powerful vehicles for communicating spiritual truths. They allow authors to express complex ideas in relatable terms, making the Divine more accessible to the reader. For example, the metaphor of the shepherd and the sheep, often used in religious texts, illustrates the relationship between God and humanity. It evokes feelings of care, guidance, and protection, emphasizing the nurturing aspect of the divine. This metaphor not only shapes our understanding of God, but also influences how we perceive our own role within the spiritual narrative. By engaging with these metaphors, we are invited to reflect on our relationship with the divine and our responsibilities as individuals within a larger community.

The language of God also shapes our perception of the divine in significant ways. The words we use to describe God influence our understanding of His nature and attributes. For example, referring to God as "Father" evokes notions of authority, protection, and love, while describing God as "Judge" can evoke feelings of fear and accountability. These linguistic choices shape our emotional responses and can foster either a sense of intimacy or distance in our relationship with the Divine.

It is important to note that God always holds us accountable for our mistakes, especially when they involve selfish choices. This recognition of accountability highlights the importance of language in shaping our understanding of divine justice and mercy. But the interpretation of spiritual texts is often influenced by the cultural and historical contexts in which they were written. Language is not static; it evolves over time, reflecting the values, beliefs, and experiences of the society that produces it. As a result, the meanings of symbols and metaphors can change, leading to different interpretations of the same text. This dynamic nature of language invites readers to engage critically with spiritual texts, encouraging them to explore the underlying messages and their relevance to contemporary life.

The ability to discern the layers of meaning within these texts fosters a deeper connection to the divine and encourages personal growth. However, relying on language to convey spiritual truths also presents challenges. The limitations of human language can lead to misunderstandings and misinterpretations of the divine. Words can be inadequate to capture the fullness of divine experience, resulting in a sense of disconnection or alienation. We should remember that the mind does not learn what it needs to learn, but rather what it chooses to learn. Thus, individuals must actively engage with language and meaning in order to discover their own truths.

Chapter 18: God and Personal Responsibility

The essence of our spiritual journey is not merely seeking divine intervention or understanding the nature of God; it is fundamentally about recognizing our role in the grand design of life. Every action we take and every decision we make reflects our understanding of God and the universe, shaping not only our destiny but also the collective experience of humanity.

Central to this understanding is the principle that we are not passive recipients of fate, but active participants in the unfolding of our lives. The notion that God does not choose religions emphasizes that the divine essence transcends the boundaries of man-made doctrines. Instead, it invites us to recognize the universal truths that govern existence and urges us to cultivate a personal relationship with the divine that is rooted in self-awareness and responsibility. This relationship is not dictated by external rituals or societal expectations, but is a deeply personal journey that requires introspection and honesty.

The teachings of spiritual growth often emphasize the importance of self-awareness as a precursor to true understanding. It is through the lens of self-awareness that we can begin to see the impact of our actions on ourselves and others. As we navigate through life, we must confront the reality that our choices are not isolated events; they resonate through the fabric of the universe, affecting the lives of those around us. This interconnectedness demands a heightened sense of responsibility, as we must acknowledge that our actions can either uplift or diminish the collective spirit of humanity.

Furthermore, the idea that God blesses us with so many gifts serves as a reminder of the abundance that surrounds us. This abundance, however, is not just a matter of material wealth; it includes the gifts of resilience, creativity, and the ability to dream. When we embrace these gifts and channel them into positive action, we align ourselves with the divine flow of the universe. Conversely, when we succumb to negativity, fear, or apathy, we not only hinder our own growth, but also contribute to the collective suffering of humanity.

The path of personal responsibility requires us to confront our fears, our prejudices, and the darker aspects of our nature. As we engage in this process, we may find ourselves confronting the consequences of our past actions. Acknowledging our mistakes is not a sign of weakness, but a crucial step toward growth. It is through this recognition that we can begin to transform our experiences into valuable lessons that allow us to evolve spiritually and emotionally.

In this context, the concept of sacrifice emerges as an essential component of personal responsibility. True sacrifice is not simply about giving up something of value; it is about investing ourselves fully in the pursuit of a higher purpose. This investment often requires letting go of attachments that no longer serve our growth, whether they are relationships, material possessions, or limiting beliefs. The willingness to make such sacrifices is a testament to our commitment to spiritual evolution and our understanding of the Divine.

As we delve deeper into the relationship between God and personal responsibility, it becomes clear that our spiritual growth is inextricably linked to our capacity for empathy and compassion. People of good heart always want the happiness of others, so we must foster a sense of community and interconnectedness. When we prioritize the well-being of others, we not only elevate our own spiritual state, but also contribute to the collective healing of society.

Moreover, the journey of personal responsibility is not a solitary endeavor. It is enriched by the relationships we cultivate and the communities in which we engage. The act of sharing our insights, experiences, and struggles with others fosters a sense of belonging and support. In this shared space, we can learn from one another, challenge our perspectives, and grow together. Recognizing that we attract people to our lives with our souls reminds us of the importance of authenticity in our interactions. When we are true to ourselves, we naturally attract those who resonate with our values and aspirations.

However, accepting personal responsibility also means recognizing our limitations and the need for divine grace. While our actions and choices significantly shape our lives, the divine presence offers guidance, strength, and forgiveness. This balance between personal effort and divine grace is essential to a holistic understanding of our role in the universe.

Chapter 19: The Future of Spirituality

As we stand on the precipice of a new era, the evolution of spirituality in modern society is about to undergo profound changes. The interplay of technology and globalization is reshaping our beliefs about God and the nature of spiritual practice. In this dynamic landscape, we must navigate the complexities of human experience, recognizing that the future of spirituality is not merely a reflection of our past, but a canvas upon which we can paint new possibilities.

The rapid advancement of technology has fundamentally changed the way we connect with each other and with the Divine. The Internet, social media, and digital platforms have created a global village where ideas, beliefs, and practices can be shared instantly. This interconnectedness fosters a rich tapestry of spiritual expression, allowing individuals to explore different traditions and philosophies without the constraints of geographic boundaries. As we embrace this digital age, we find ourselves at a crossroads where traditional religious structures may be challenged and new forms of spirituality may emerge.

In this context, the role of technology goes beyond mere communication; it serves as a tool for spiritual exploration and self-discovery. Virtual reality experiences, meditation apps, and online communities provide individuals with unprecedented access to spiritual teachings and practices. This democratization of spirituality allows for a more personalized approach, where individuals can curate their spiritual journeys based on their unique needs and aspirations. However, this shift also raises questions about authenticity and the potential dilution of spiritual traditions. As we navigate this terrain, it is important to discern the genuine from the superficial, and to ensure that our spiritual pursuits remain rooted in meaningful experiences rather than fleeting trends.

Globalization also plays a central role in shaping our beliefs about God and spirituality. As cultures collide and intermingle, we are witnessing the emergence of syncretic spiritual practices that blend elements from different traditions. This fusion can lead to a richer understanding of the divine as individuals draw from a variety of beliefs to construct their spiritual identities. However, it also poses challenges, as the commercialization of spirituality can lead to the appropriation of sacred practices without a genuine understanding of their meaning. In this globalized world, we must cultivate a sense of respect and reverence for the traditions with which we engage, recognizing that spirituality is not simply a product to be consumed, but a profound journey of connection and growth.

As we look to the future, it is critical to acknowledge the shifting paradigms of faith. The rise of secularism and the questioning of traditional religious authority have led many to seek alternative spiritual paths. This search for meaning often manifests as a desire for personal empowerment and self-actualization. Individuals are increasingly turning inward, seeking to understand their own consciousness and the nature of existence. This introspective approach is consistent with teachings that emphasize the importance of self-awareness and personal responsibility in spiritual growth.

In addition, the future of spirituality is likely to be characterized by a greater emphasis on experiential knowledge over dogmatic beliefs. As individuals seek to connect with the divine, they may prioritize direct experiences of spirituality-such as meditation and immersion in nature-over adherence to prescribed doctrines. This shift reflects a growing recognition that spirituality is not confined to religious institutions, but is an inherent aspect of the human experience. The teachings remind us that the answers to everything we have ever wanted have always been within us. This inner exploration fosters a sense of empowerment, encouraging individuals to trust their intuition and embrace their unique spiritual paths.

In this evolving landscape, the concept of community will also change. As traditional religious congregations decline, new forms of spiritual community are emerging, often facilitated by technology. Online forums, social media groups, and virtual gatherings allow individuals to connect with like-minded seekers, fostering a sense of belonging and shared purpose. These communities can serve as support systems, providing encouragement and inspiration as individuals navigate their spiritual journeys. However, it is important to approach these virtual connections with discernment, ensuring that they contribute positively to our growth rather than perpetuating negativity or division.

As we consider the future of spirituality, we must also consider the ethical implications of our beliefs and practices. In an age marked by social and environmental challenges, spirituality can serve as a catalyst for positive change, inspiring individuals to engage in acts of compassion, justice, and stewardship. By recognizing our interconnectedness and responsibility to one another and to the planet, we can cultivate a spirituality that transcends individualism and promotes collective well-being.

Chapter 20: Embracing the Divine

In the search for spiritual fulfillment, a relationship with the Divine is a fundamental aspect of the human experience. More than an act of faith, embracing the Divine is a profound journey that invites individuals to explore their spirituality beyond the confines of dogma. This exploration is especially important in a world where traditional beliefs are often challenged and the search for personal meaning is increasingly important. To deepen this relationship with God, one must take practical steps that foster connection, understanding, and growth.

The first step in this journey is to cultivate self-knowledge. Self-awareness is not just about recognizing one's thoughts and feelings; it is about understanding the underlying motivations and desires that drive our actions. Practices such as meditation or contemplative prayer can create a space for introspection. This introspection helps to identify the spiritual impulses that guide us, as well as the ego-driven desires that can lead us astray. The journey to self-knowledge is an ongoing one that requires patience and commitment, but it is essential for anyone seeking a deeper connection with the Divine.

Once self-awareness is established, the next step is to embrace the practice of gratitude. Gratitude is a powerful tool for spiritual growth because it shifts our focus from what we lack to the abundance that surrounds us. Spiritual teachings remind us that God blesses us with so many gifts that it is, in a sense, ungrateful of us to suffer. By acknowledging and appreciating the blessings in our lives, we open ourselves to a greater understanding of the divine presence. This practice can be as simple as keeping a gratitude journal to record daily blessings or taking time each day to reflect on the positive aspects of life. In this way, we cultivate a mindset that is receptive to divine guidance and inspiration.

In addition, engaging with nature can greatly enhance our spiritual connection. Nature has long been seen as a reflection of the divine, a manifestation of God's creativity and power. Spending time in natural settings allows individuals to experience a sense of peace and connection that is often elusive in the hustle and bustle of daily life. Spiritual teachings suggest that once you understand spirituality for what it is, religion gradually loses its importance in your life. This understanding encourages individuals to seek the divine in the world around them, recognizing that the beauty of creation is a direct reflection of the Creator. Whether through hiking, gardening, or simply sitting in a park, immersion in nature can foster a deeper appreciation for the divine presence in everyday life.

In addition to self-awareness and gratitude, it is important to explore personal spirituality beyond dogma. Many people feel constrained by the rigid structures of organized religion, which can stifle personal growth and exploration. Spiritual teachings emphasize that the main difference between religion and spirituality is that religion is what you are told, and spirituality is what you seek. This distinction invites individuals to break free from the confines of dogma and engage in a more personal and authentic spiritual practice. This exploration may involve studying different spiritual traditions, engaging in discussions with other spiritual seekers, or simply allowing oneself to ask questions and seek answers without fear of judgment.

In addition, the practice of compassion and service to others is an important aspect of embracing the divine. By extending kindness and compassion to others, we not only uplift those around us, but also deepen our connection to the Divine. Acts of service can take many forms, from volunteering in the community to simply offering a listening ear to a friend in need. These acts create a ripple effect of positivity and love, reinforcing the understanding that we are all interconnected in the divine tapestry of life.

As individuals embark on this journey of embracing the Divine, it is essential to remain open to the unexpected. Spiritual teachings emphasize that all the sounds, words, emotions, and memories of past experiences cannot adequately prepare us for encounters with the unexpected. Life is full of surprises, and it is often in these moments of uncertainty that we encounter profound spiritual insights. By cultivating an attitude of openness and curiosity, we allow ourselves to be guided by the divine in ways we may not have anticipated.

Glossary of Terms

Accountability: The responsibility to act in accordance with one's beliefs and values, often reinforced by community and divine judgment.

Alignment: The process of bringing one's actions and intentions into harmony with divine principles.

Belief: A conviction or acceptance that something is true, often shaped by religious or spiritual teachings.

Belonging: The sense of connection and community that comes from shared beliefs and practices.

Compassion: The ability to empathize with others and respond with kindness and understanding, reflecting divine love.

Community: A group of people who share common beliefs, values, and spiritual practices, fostering a sense of belonging and support.

Consciousness: The awareness of one's thoughts, emotions, and actions that connects individuals to the Divine and the universe.

Creativity: The expression of one's unique gifts and talents that reflect the divine spark within.

Divine: The essence of God, a universal principle that governs the cosmos and is manifested in all beings.

Divine Judgement: The belief that individuals will be held accountable for their actions by a higher power.

Divine Love: The unconditional love that permeates all aspects of life and reflects the nature of God.

Divine Will: The dynamic force that guides existence and allows for free will and creativity.

Dogma: Rigid beliefs or doctrines that can hinder personal spiritual growth.

Ego: The construct that thrives on the perception of individuality and separation, often leading to a false narrative of isolation.

Emotions: The feelings that connect us to the divine and shape our spiritual experiences.

Empathy: The ability to understand and share the feelings of another, fostering compassion and connection.

Enlightenment: A state of spiritual awakening and understanding, often achieved through self-awareness and introspection.

Evil: A deviation from the divine order, often seen as a consequence of human free will.

Faith: A deep-seated belief and trust in a greater purpose that guides individuals through life's uncertainties and challenges.

Fear: An emotion that can cloud our perception of the divine and lead us to believe in a punishing rather than a loving God.

Free Will: The ability to make choices and act with intention, shaping our experiences and spiritual growth.

God: The central concept in human thought that transcends cultures, eras, and belief systems, embodying principles of love, compassion, and interconnectedness.

Gratitude: The practice of acknowledging and appreciating the blessings in one's life, which fosters a deeper connection to the Divine.

Human Potential: The vast potential within each individual, unleashed through recognition of the Divine and personal responsibility.

Illusion of Separation: The belief that we are separate from God and from each other, which fosters a sense of isolation and disconnection.

Introspection: The practice of self-examination and reflection that leads to greater self-knowledge and spiritual growth.

Interconnectedness: The fundamental aspect of understanding God, recognizing that all beings are part of a greater whole.

Judgment: The process of being held accountable for one's actions, often associated with divine intervention and moral responsibility.

Justice: The principle of fairness and equity, often seen as a reflection of divine will and a call to action for social responsibility.

Goodness: The act of showing compassion and understanding that reflects divine love and fosters connectedness.

Love: The highest expression of the divine, a force that transcends the ordinary and connects us to the essence of existence.

Meditation: A practice that promotes quieting the mind and connecting with one's inner self, allowing for a deeper understanding of the Divine.

Morality: The principles that guide ethical behavior, often based on divine teachings and personal responsibility.

Nature: The manifestation of divine creativity and power, often seen as a reflection of the Creator.

Personal Responsibility: The recognition of one's role in the grand design of life, shaping one's destiny through actions and choices.

Prayer: A profound practice that serves as a bridge between the human mind and the divine, fostering a deeper understanding of oneself and one's place in the universe.

Resilience: The ability to face and overcome challenges, often fostered by faith and a sense of divine support.

Responsibility: The sense of accountability that encourages individuals to align their behavior with their spiritual values.

Sacrifice: The willingness to invest oneself fully in the pursuit of a higher purpose, often requiring the sacrifice of personal comfort.

Self-awareness: The ability to observe one's thoughts, emotions, and actions without judgment, leading to greater insight and spiritual growth.

Self-Discovery: The journey of exploring one's inner self, recognizing the divine spark within.

Service: Acts of kindness and compassion that uplift others and deepen one's connection to the divine.

Spiritual Growth: The process of personal and spiritual development, often achieved through introspection and self-awareness.

Spirituality: A personal and subjective experience of the divine, often involving personal spiritual experiences and practices.

Suffering: An intrinsic part of the human condition that often serves as a catalyst for spiritual awakening and personal transformation.

Transformation: The process of profound change, often achieved through self-awareness, introspection, and recognition of the divine within.

Truth: The dynamic, evolving understanding of existence, shaped by experiences, beliefs, and insights gained along the way.

Unconditional Love: The divine love that pervades all aspects of life, transcending conditions and expectations.

Understanding: The process of gaining insight into one's true self and the nature of the Divine.

Virtues: The qualities that reflect divine attributes, often cultivated through personal responsibility and ethical behavior.

Vulnerability: The willingness to face one's fears and insecurities, allowing for personal growth and spiritual transformation.

Wisdom: The knowledge and understanding gained through personal observation, insight, and experience that leads to spiritual growth.

Zeal: The enthusiasm and passion that drive individuals to pursue their dreams and aspirations, often inspired by the realization of the divine.

Book Review Request

Dear reader,

Thank you for purchasing this book! I would love to know your opinion. Writing a book review helps in understanding the readers and also impacts other readers' purchasing decisions. Your opinion matters. Please write a book review!

Your kindness is greatly appreciated!

About the Author

Dan Desmarques is a renowned author with a remarkable track record in the literary world. With an impressive portfolio of 28 Amazon bestsellers, including eight #1 bestsellers, Dan is a respected figure in the industry. Drawing on his background as a college professor of academic and creative writing, as well as his experience as a seasoned business consultant, Dan brings a unique blend of expertise to his work. His profound insights and transformational content appeal to a wide audience, covering topics as diverse as personal growth, success, spirituality, and the deeper meaning of life. Through his writing, Dan empowers readers to break free from limitations, unlock their inner potential, and embark on a journey of self-discovery and transformation. In a competitive self-help market, Dan's exceptional talent and inspiring stories make him a standout author, motivating readers to engage with his books and embark on a path of personal growth and enlightenment.

Also Written by the Author

1. 66 Days to Change Your Life: 12 Steps to Effortlessly Remove Mental Blocks, Reprogram Your Brain and Become a Money Magnet

2. A New Way of Being: How to Rewire Your Brain and Take Control of Your Life

3. Abnormal: How to Train Yourself to Think Differently and Permanently Overcome Evil Thoughts

4. Alignment: The Process of Transmutation Within the Mechanics of Life

5. Audacity: How to Make Fast and Efficient Decisions in Any Situation

6. Beyond Belief: Discovering Sacred Moments in Everyday Life

7. Beyond Illusions: Discovering Your True Nature

8. Beyond Self-Doubt: Unleashing Boundless Confidence for Extraordinary Living

9. Breaking Free from Samsara: Achieving Spiritual Liberation and Inner Peace

10. Breakthrough: Embracing Your True Potential in a Changing World

11. Christ Cult Codex: The Untold Secrets of the Abrahamic Religions and the Cult of Jesus

12. Codex Illuminatus: Quotes & Sayings of Dan Desmarques

13. Collective Consciousness: How to Transcend Mass Consciousness and Become One With the Universe

14. Creativity: Everything You Always Wanted to Know About How to Use Your Imagination to Create Original Art That People Admire

15. Deception: When Everything You Know about God is Wrong

16. Demigod: What Happens When You Transcend The Human Nature?

17. Discernment: How Do Your Emotions Affect Moral Decision-Making?

18. Design Your Dream Life: A Guide to Living Purposefully

19. Eclipsing Mediocrity: How to Unveil Hidden Realities and Master Life's Challenges

20. Energy Vampires: How to Identify and Protect Yourself

21. Fearless: Powerful Ways to Get Abundance Flowing into Your Life

22. Feel, Think and Grow Rich: 4 Elements to Attract Success in Life

23. Find More with Less: Uncluttering Your Mind, Body, and Soul

24. Find Your Flow: How to Get Wisdom and Knowledge from God

25. Hacking the Universe: The Revolutionary Way to Achieve Your Dreams and Unleash Your True Power

26. Holistic Psychology: 77 Secrets about the Mind That They Don't Want You to Know

27. How to Change the World: The Path of Global Ascension Through Consciousness

28. How to Get Lucky: How to Change Your Mind and Get Anything in Life

29. How to Improve Your Self-Esteem: 34 Essential Life Lessons Everyone Should Learn to Find Genuine Happiness

30. How to Study and Understand Anything: Discovering The Secrets of the Greatest Geniuses in History

31. How to Spot and Stop Manipulators: Protecting Yourself and Reclaiming Your Life

32. Intuition: 5 Keys to Awaken Your Third Eye and Expand Spiritual Perception

33. Karma Mastery: Transforming Life's Lessons into Conscious Creations

34. Legacy: How to Build a Life Worth Remembering

35. Master Your Emotions: The Art of Intentional Living

36. Mastering Alchemy: The Key to Success and Spiritual Growth

37. Metanoia Mechanics: The Secret Science of Profound Mental Shifts

38. Metamorphosis: 16 Catalysts for Unconventional Growth and Transformation

39. Mindshift: Aligning Your Thoughts for a Better Life

40. Mind Over Madness: Strategies for Thriving Amidst Chaos

41. Money Matters: A Holistic Approach to Building Financial Freedom and Well-Being

42. Quantum Leap: Unleashing Your Infinite Potential

43. Religious Leadership: The 8 Rules Behind Successful Congregations

44. Reset: How to Observe Life Through the Hidden Dimensions of Reality and Change Your Destiny

45. Resilience: The Art of Confronting Reality Against the Odds

46. Raise Your Frequency: Aligning with Higher Consciousness

47. Revelation: The War Between Wisdom and Human Perception

48. Spiritual Anarchist: Breaking the Chains of Consensual Delusion

49. Spiritual DNA: Bridging Science and Spirituality to Live Your Best Life

50. Spiritual Warfare: What You Need to Know About Overcoming Adversity

51. Starseed: Secret Teachings about Heaven and the Future of Humanity

52. Stupid People: Identifying, Analyzing and Overcoming Their Toxic Influence

53. Technocracy: The New World Order of the Illuminati

and The Battle Between Good and Evil

54. The 10 Laws of Transmutation: The Multidimensional Power of Your Subconscious Mind

55. The 14 Karmic Laws of Love: How to Develop a Healthy and Conscious Relationship With Your Soulmate

56. The 33 Laws of Persistence: How to Overcome Obstacles and Upgrade Your Mindset for Success

57. The 36 Laws of Happiness: How to Solve Urgent Problems and Create a Better Future

58. The Alchemy of Truth: Embracing Change and Transcending Time

59. The Altruistic Edge: Succeeding by Putting Others First

60. The Antagonists: What Makes a Successful Person Different?

61. The Antichrist: The Grand Plan of Total Global Enslavement

62. The Art of Letting Go: Embracing Uncertainty and Living a Fulfilling Life

63. The Awakening: How to Turn Darkness Into Light and Ascend to Higher Dimensions of Existence

64. The Egyptian Mysteries: Essential Hermetic Teachings for a Complete Spiritual Reformation

65. The Dark Side of Progress: Navigating the Pitfalls of Technology and Society

66. The Evil Within: The Spiritual Battle in Your Mind Deception: When Everything You Know about God is Wrong

67. The Game of Life and How to Play It: How to Get Anything You Want in Life

68. The Hidden Language of God: How to Find a Balance Between Freedom and Responsibility

69. The Mosaic of Destiny: Deciphering the Patterns of Your Life

70. The Most Powerful Quotes: 400 Motivational Quotes and Sayings

71. The Multidimensional Nature of Reality: Transcending the Limits of the Human Mind

72. The Secret Beliefs of The Illuminati: The Complete Truth About Manifesting Money Using The Law of Attraction That is Being Hidden From You

73. The Secret Empire: The Hidden Truth Behind the Power Elite and the Knights of the New World Order

74. The Secret Science of the Soul: How to Transcend Common Sense and Get What You Really Want From Life

75. The Spiritual Laws of Money: The 31 Best-kept Secrets to Life-long Abundance

76. The Spiritual Mechanics of Love: Secrets They Don't Want You to Know about Understanding and Processing Emotions

77. The Universal Code: Understanding the Divine Blueprint

78. The Unknown: Exploring Infinite Possibilities in a Conformist World

79. The Narcissist's Secret: Why They Hate You (and What to Do About It)

80. Thrive: Spark Creativity, Overcome Obstacles and Unleash Your Potential

81. Transcend: Embracing Change and Overcoming Life's Challenges

82. Uncharted Paths: Pursuing True Fulfillment Beyond Society's Expectations

83. Uncompromised: The Surprising Power of Integrity in a Corrupt World

84. Unacknowledged: How Negative Emotions Affect Your Mental Health?

85. Unapologetic: Taking Control of Your Mind for a

Happier and Healthier Life

86. Unbreakable: Turning Hardship into Opportunity

87. Uncommon: Transcending the Lies of the Mental Health Industry

88. Unlocked: How to Get Answers from Your Subconscious Mind and Control Your Life

89. Why do good people suffer? Uncovering the Hidden Dynamics of Human Nature

90. Your Full Potential: How to Overcome Fear and Solve Any Problem

91. Your Soul Purpose: Reincarnation and the Spectrum of Consciousness in Human Evolution

About the Publisher

This book was published by 22 Lions Publishing.

www.22Lions.com

Printed in the USA
CPSIA information can be obtained
at www.ICGtesting.com
LVHW021149071124
795952LV00012B/523